Paverpol World Art

Jossy de Roode

Colofon

samenstelling/compilation:
Jossy de Roode, Netherlands, Josefine Art www.josefine-art.com

uitgeverij/publisher:
Paverpol Art Products International, Netherlands, www.paverpol.com

druk/print: De Grootdruk, Netherlands

Inhouds opgave / Contents

Inleiding / introduction   **6 & 7**

Lennie Adams,	USA	8 & 9
Manolis Apostolakis,	Greece	10
Art Atelier,	Switzerland	11 & 12
Silvia Aujeska,	Slovakia	13
Carla Bellou,	Greece	62 & 63
Dina Blot,	Canada	14 & 15
Ina Boer,	Netherlands	16 & 17
Sue Cherry,	Australia	18
Lizzie Ciesluk,	Canada	19, 20 & 21
Eileen Crandall,	Canada	22 & 23
Mary Lou Devine,	Canada	52
Tzia Dimopoulou,	Greece	24 & 25
Sue Gaffy,	Australia	26 & 27
Annet Holierhoek,	Canada	28 & 29
Trijntje Huizinga,	Denmark	30 & 31
IAM,	France	32
Sue Josling,	United Kingdom	33
Denise Keeley,	Australia	34
Katja Kleinova,	Slovakia	35, 36 & 37
Herman Kluck,	Canada	38 & 39
Thecla Kluck,	Canada	40
Lon Korpershoek,	Greece	41 & 42
Janice Laurent,	Australia	43 & 44
Christa Light,	USA	45, 46 & 47
Joane Leduc,	Canada	48 & 49
Sandy Little,	USA	50 & 51
Beata Madova,	Slovakia	53
Suus Manhave,	Netherlands	54 & 55
Lynette Matheim,	Australia	56
Jorgelina Maria Melis,	Italy	57, 58 & 59
Genie Morgan,	USA	60 & 61
Caty Navarro Fierro,	Mexico	64 & 65

Gwen Nicholson,	New Zealand	66 & 67
Irini Penna,	Greece	68
Gloria Perry,	North Ireland	69, 70 & 71
Jana Petova,	Czech Republique	72 & 73
Eef Pieterman,	Netherlands	74, 75 & 76
Jossy de Roode,	Netherlands	77 & 78
Joanne Savage,	Canada	79
Ingrid Schouten,	Netherlands	80 & 81
Maria Schultz,	USA	82 & 83
Amanda Seales,	United Kingdom	84
Jin-Ok-Shin,	South Korea	85 & 86
Rosa Sirvient,	Spain	87 & 88
Sinelli,	Finland	89
Riëtte Smit,	Netherlands	90, 91 & 92
Lex Sorrentino,	Australia	93 & 94
Lise St-Cyr,	Canada	95 & 96
Edina Szilardi,	Hungary	97
Shirley Tasker,	United Kingdom	98 & 99
Merilyn Thomas,	Australia	100 & 101
Liliane van Tilborgh,	Belgium	102 & 103
Brenda Topley,	Canada	104 & 105
Jantina Tuthill,	USA	106
Toos Vermeulen,	Netherlands	107, 108 & 109
Elena Vylegzhanina,	Russia	110 & 111
Suus van de Water,	Netherlands	112
Harlinde Wieërs,	Belgium	113, 114 & 115
Iris Willems,	Belgium	116 & 117
Kim Willoughby,	Australia	118 & 119
Helle Winther,	Denmark	120 & 121
Monika Zilkova,	Czech Republique	122 & 123

Wat is Paverpol?   **124**
What is Paverpol?   **125**
Paverpol importers list per country   **126 & 127**

Inleiding

Dit boek is tot stand gekomen met medewerking van 62 Paverpol kunstenaars, uit alle delen van de wereld. Ik dank hen hierbij allemaal voor het sturen van foto's van hun werkstukken. Het was een feest om ze te bekijken, te selecteren en een groot aantal voor dit boek te gebruiken.

Alle kunstenaressen in dit boek hebben hun werkstukken gemaakt met Paverpol vormpolymeer. Een vloeistof waarmee allerhande materialen keihard en buitenbestendig gemaakt kunnen worden. Met name textiel.

Laat dit boek u inspireren tot het maken van prachtige werkstukken. Met Paverpol vormpolymeer gaat het u zeker lukken. Jong en oud kunnen met dit milieuvriendelijke product de mooiste werkstukken maken. De mogelijkheden zijn legio.
Informatie over werkwijze en gebruik van materialen bij de werkstukken, kunt u bij de betreffende kunstenaar opvragen.

Veel kijk- en leesplezier,

Jossy de Roode

Introduction

This book came about thanks to the co-operation of 62 Paverpol artists from every corner of the globe. I would like to take this opportunity to thank all of them for sending in photographs of their work. It was a real treat to view these and to select and use quite a number of pieces of work for this book.

All of the (female) artists in this book used Paverpol shaping polymer to create their pieces of work. It is a fluid that can be used to render all kinds of material rock hard and weather-resistant. Particularly textile.

Let this book inspire you to create lovely pieces of work. You will certainly succeed if you use Paverpol shaping polymer. Both young and old can use this environment-friendly product to create the most beautiful works. There is no end to the possibilities.

You can request information on the method of working and the use of the materials for these pieces of work from the artist concerned.

We wish you much viewing and reading pleasure.

Jossy de Roode

Lennie Adams

Forming

Aquarius

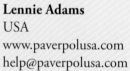

Lennie Adams
USA
www.paverpolusa.com
help@paverpolusa.com

Manolis Apostolakis

Manolis Apostolakis,
tel. (+30)280327487
Heraklion Crete Greece

Birds with Hearts

Art Atelier

Rusty Balls

Flower Decoration

Art Atelier
Ottikon Switzerland
info@art-atelier.ch

Angel

Silvia Aujeska
Slovakia,
www.paverpol.sk
info@paverpol.sk

Dina Blot

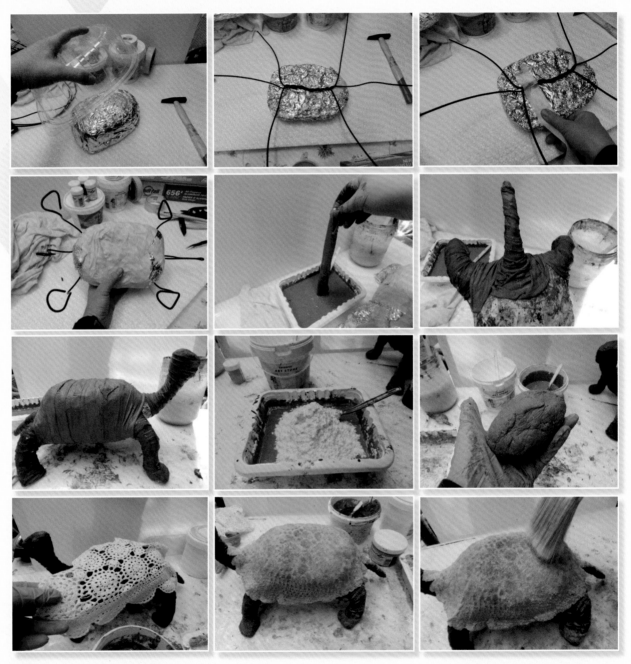

Construction Turtle

Dina Blot

Dina Blot
Canada
dinablot@bellaliant.net

Ina Boer

Materials: Paverpol black, Wrappers, Pavercotton, armature, tin foil, 1 old T-shirt, lace, masking tape, acrylic paint Bronze, little piece of board, cord.

Ina Boer

Jasmin on Swing

Ina Boer
Netherlands
ina.boer@hotmail.com
www.veranda-paverpol.nl

Sue Cherry

Sue Cherry
Australia
suchgardenart@bigpond.com
www.such-garden-art.weebly.co

Lizzie Ciesluk

Springtime in Paris

Lizzie Ciesluk

Dominica

Lizzie Ciesluk

Copper Mermaid

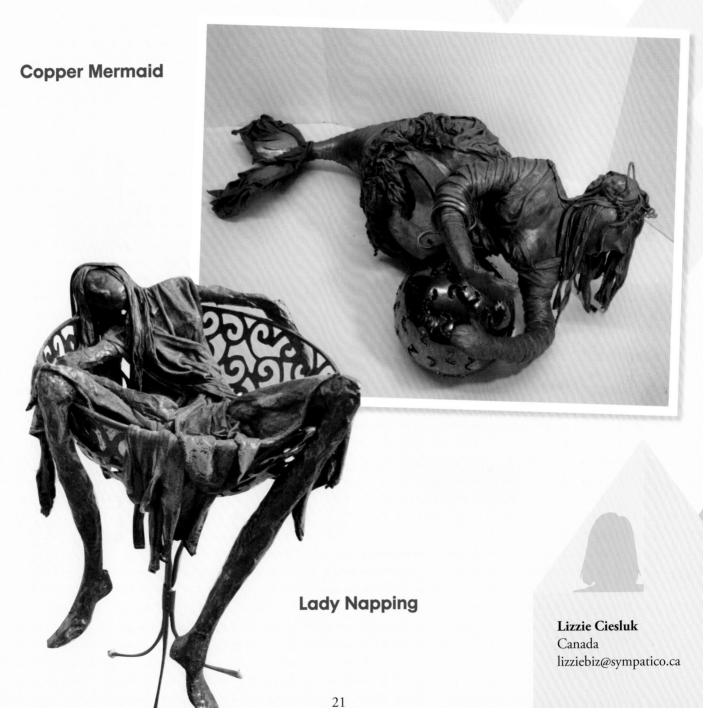

Lady Napping

Lizzie Ciesluk
Canada
lizziebiz@sympatico.ca

Eileen Crandall

Materials Mushroom:
Paverpol transparent, Paverplast, Josefine Varnish, Acrylic paint Brown, Styrofoam circles, tin foil

Materials Fairy: Paverpol Black and Transparent, Paverplast, Wrappers, Pavercolor Brown, Pavercotton, Reliëfdecoration, Josefine Varnish, air dry clay, Die cut wings

Eileen Crandall

Paverpol Garden Fairy

Eileen Crandall
Canada
www.inspired2create.ca

23

Tzia Dimopoulou

Materials: Paverpol transparent, Electricity cable, balloon, little mask to make the face, tin foil, rice paper, textile, iron wire, socket and flex

Lamp

Tzia Dimopoulou

Medusa

Materials: Paverpol Black, Art Stone, Pavercolors Sea Blue and Silver, Chicken wire, old journals, tin foil, textile, pin with base, acrylic paint Silver, electricity cable, mask mold, air dry clay

Tzia Dimopoulou
Greece
tziadimo@gmail.com

Sue Gaffy

Materials: Paverpol Transparent, Pavercolor, Wrappers, Pavercotton, wood, dowels, chicken wire, air dry clay, polystyrene ball, tin foil

Sue Gaffy
Australia
inazoodesigns@live.com.au
www.inazoodesigns.bigpixie.com

Annet Holierhoek

**Art Stone Birds
with long legs**

Materials: Paverpol Black or
Lead Grey, Paverplast, Pavercolor
Jeans Blue and Mother of Pearl,
Art Stone, tin foil, masking tape,
2 kebab sticks, pliers, Hair spray
or Spray varnish.

One Size More

Materials: Paverpol Bronze and Black, Paverplast, Pavercolor Antique Gold, Wrappers, Josefine Varnish, electrical wire, piece of foam, Masking Tape, tin foil, Styrofoam balls

Construction One size more

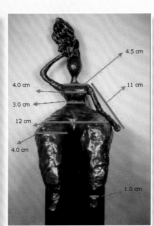

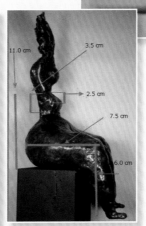

Annet Holierhoek
Canada
info@paverpol.ca
www.paverpol.ca
www.orangewireart.ca

Trijntje Huizinga

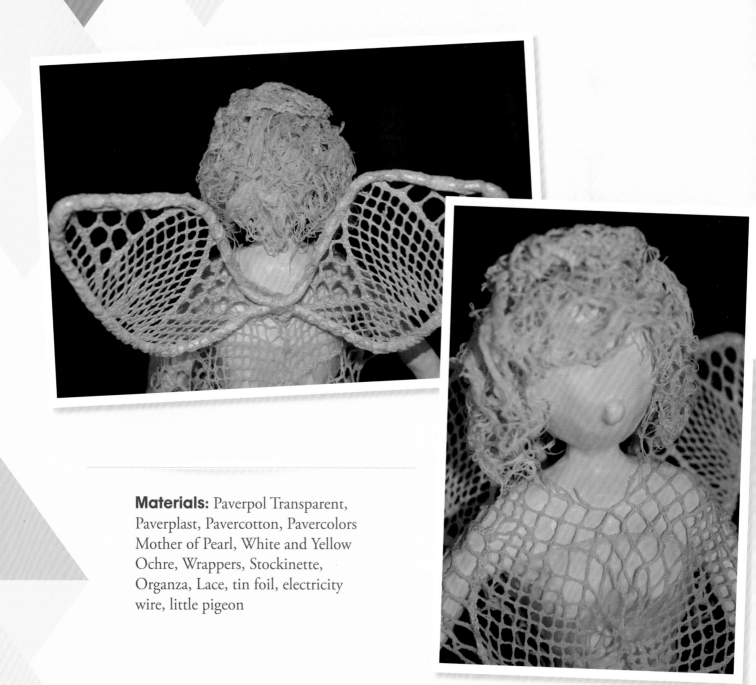

Materials: Paverpol Transparent, Paverplast, Pavercotton, Pavercolors Mother of Pearl, White and Yellow Ochre, Wrappers, Stockinette, Organza, Lace, tin foil, electricity wire, little pigeon

Angel

Trijntje Huizinga
Denmark
www.trijntjesdesign.dk

IAM

Les Triplettes

IAM,
France
www.iam-sculpture.com

Harry the Hare

Materials: Paverpol Lead Grey,
Paverplast, Wrappers

Sue Josling
United Kingdom
enquiries@paverpol-uk.co.uk

Denise Keeley

Materials: Paverpol Transparent, Pavercolor Terra Cotta, Art Stone, Textile, Paper Mask

Denise Keeley
Australia
denise@paverpolaustralia.com
www.paverpolaustralia.com

Katja Kleinova

Dancing Hares

Construction

35

Katja Kleinova

Construction Lady with a dog

Lady with a dog

Katja Kleinova
Slovakia
info@paverpol.sk
www.paverpol.sk

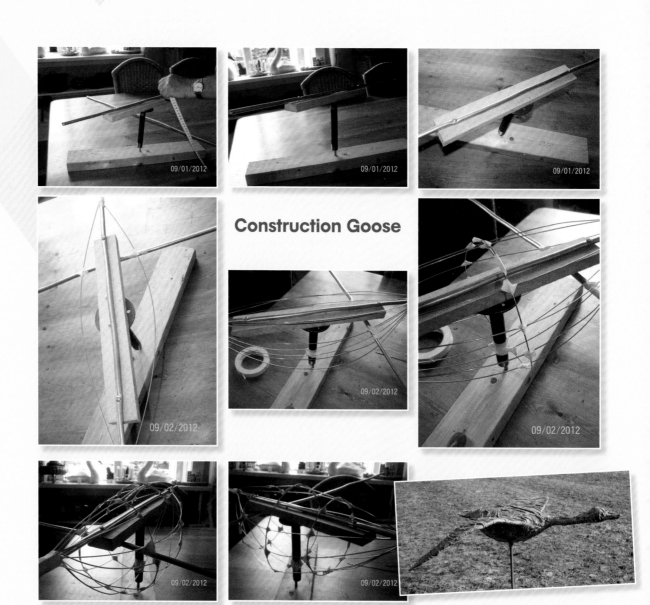

Construction Goose

09/01/2012

09/02/2012

Goose

Herman Kluck
Canada
kluckdutchhill@jcis.ca
www.thedutchhill.com

Thecla Kluck

Dreamer

Thecla Kluck
Canada
theclakluck@hotmail.com
www.thedutchhill.com

Lon Korpershoek

Flower Girl in the Garden

Materials: Paverpol Black, air dry clay, Styrofoam ball, tin foil, iron wire, textile

Lon Korpershoek

Flower Girl

Lon Korpershoek
Greece
paverpol@carlabellou.gr

Janice Laurent

Little Warrior

Materials: Paverpol,
Pavercolors, Art Stone,
Polymer clay, sand, timber,
tin foil, textile

Janice Laurent

Angel

Materials: Paverpol
Transparent, recycled
fabrics

Janice Laurent
Australia
janice.laurent@bigpond.com
www.laurentlessartdolls.com

Christa Light

MS Horse

Christa Light

Baby and Shoes

Pregnant woman

Pavercats

Christa Light

Dragon

Crackle Mask

Mask

Christa Light
USA
www.paverpolusa.com
help@paverpolusa.com

Joane Leduc

Victor Le Centaure

Joane Leduc

Bibi Contrebasse

Joane Leduc
Canada
joaneleducart@yahoo.com
www.joaneleducart.blogspot.com

Sandy Little

Mermaid

Silk Paper Project

Sleeper

Sandy Little
USA
www.paverpolusa.com
help@paverpolusa.com

Mary Lou Devine

Flow'rs in the Snow

Mary Lou Devine
Canada
maryloudevine@gmail.com
www.simplydevinepaverpol.co

Violet Flowers

Beata Madova
Slovakia
info@paverpol.sk
www.paverpol.sk

Suus Manhave

Materials: Paverpol Transparent,
canvas, pieces of fabric, sand,
masks, tin foil, cat bells

Suus Manhave

Harlequin

Suus Manhave
Netherlands
suusadri@hotmail.com

Lynette Matheim

Eli Bird

Lynette Matheim
Australia
lmathein@y7mail.com

Jorgelina Maria Melis

Tango Dancers

Maricarmen

Materials Tango Dancers:
Paverpol Bronze and Transparent,
Art Stone, Stockinette,
Pavercotton, Acrylic paint Violet,
Silver, Pink, Red, Gold,
Turquoise, Varnish

Materials Maricarmen:
Paverpol Bronze, Cotton,
Stockinette, Acrylic paint
Red, Gold, Varnish

Jorgelina Maria Melis

The World

Materials The World: Paverpol
Bronze, Stockinette, Pavercotton,
Acrylic paint Gold, Varnish

Time

Materials Time: Paverpol
Transparent, Pavercolor Dark
Green, Art Stone,
Reliëfdecoration, Acrylic paint
Gold and Red, Varnish

Jorgelina Maria Melis

Luana

Materials Luana: Paverpol
Bronze, Art Stone, Cotton,
Acrylic paint Violet, Silver,
Turquoise, Varnish

Jorgelina Maria Melis
Italia
jorgymelis@hotmail.it
facebook: jorgelina melis sculptor

Genie Morgan

Emerging Cross

Genie Morgan

Run of the Horses

Watered Wall

Genie Morgan
USA
www.paverpolusa.com
help@paverpolusa.com

Carla Bellou

Construction Dragon

Carla Bellou

Red Dragon

Carla Bellou
Greece
paverpol@carlabellou.gr
www.paverpol.gr

Maria and Flowers

Cleo

Caty Navarro Fierro
Mexico
cnavarro@fresho2.com
www.fresho2.com

Gwen Nicholson

Chook

Materials: Paverpol Black, Art Stone, Stockinette, driftwood, polystyrene scraps, tin foil, T-shirt strips, beads, Bronze paint

Oscar

Extended Family

Materials Oscar: Paverpol Bronze, Paverplast, Wrappers, Art Stone, aluminium garden cane, PVC drainpipe, tin foil, Soft Bronze paint

Materials Extended Family: Paverpol Black, Art Stone, Polysterene base, driftwood, Soft Bronze paint

Gwen Nicholson
New Zealand
gwen@beefree.co.nz
www.beefreecreations.co.nz

Irini Penna

Materials: Paverpol transparent, Stockinette, chicken wire, stones and shells

Irini Penna
Greece
irinipenna@gmail.com

Gloria Perry

Gloria with Large Lady and Child

Gloria Perry

Lunantishee Elves

Ladies in White

George and Georgina Gandering Home

Detail of George

Materials George and Georgina: Paverpol Black, old bed sheet and an old cotton T-shirt, metal rods, polystyrene balls, masking tape, electrical wire, tin foil, strong wire, Acrylic paints Viridian Hue, Grass Green, Silver, Bronze, Gold

Gloria Perry
N. Ireland
gloria@urneycreations.co.uk
www.urneycreations.co.uk

Jana Petova

Sara

Jana Petova

Standing in the Wind

Jana Petova
Czech Republique
www.paverpol.sk
info@paverpol.sk

Eef Pieterman

Materials: Paverpol Bronze, Paverplast, Wrappers, Art Stone, electrical wire, metal pin with base, cotton T-shirt, Styropor cone, tin foil, masking tape, Acrylic paints Raw Umber, Oxide Green, Bronze

Allied

Eef Pieterman

Relax

Materials: Paverpol Bronze, Paverplast, Art Stone, Pavercolor Brown, tin foil, electrical wire, masking tape, planks

Eef Pieterman

Violet

Materials: Paverpol Transparent, Pavercolor White and Light Brown, Pavercotton, Wrappers, electrical wire, metal pin with base, tin foil, Masking tape, fabrics, lace, Acrylic paint Rose Madder, Titanium White, Sand Gold

Eef Pieterman
Netherlands
www.evasatelierbreda.nl
evasatelierbreda@gmail.com

Jossy de Roode

Family

Materials: Paverpol Transparent, Pavercolor Dark Green, Reliëfdecoration, old cotton T-shirts, Felt, plaster heads, metal pins with bases, acrylic paints Green, White, Gold, Bronze

Jossy de Roode

Tree of Freedom

Materials: Paverpol Black, Paverplast,
Wrappers, Reliëfdecoration, tin foil, electrical
wire, masking tape, metal pin with base acrylic
paint Gold and Bronze

Jossy de Roode
Netherlands
www.josefine-art.com

Joanne Savaga

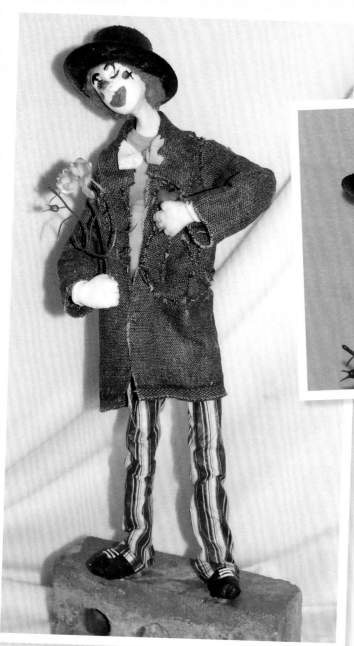

Clown

Joanne Savage
Canada
joanne.savage@hotmail.com
www.paverpoljoannesavage.
blogspot.com

Ingrid Schouten

Solidarity

Materials: Paverpol Black, Paverplast, Wrappers, electrical wire,tin foil, masking tape, Acrylic paint Bronze, Varnish, stone, metal pin

Ingrid Schouten

Fighting with the Storm

Materials: Paverpol Black, Paverplast, Art Stone, Pavercotton, Wrappers, Stockinette, electrical wire, Tin Foil, stone, metal pin, masking tape, cotton T-shirt, little umbrella, Acrylic paint Green, Violet, Bronze, Gold

Ingrid Schouten
Netherlands
schouteningrid@hotmail.com

Maria Schultz

Dragon

Maria Schultz

Animal Hangups

Maria Schultz
Canada
www.queenofarts.blogspot.com

Amanda Seales

Bronze Fairy

Amanda Seales
United Kingdom
mandyseales@yahoo.co.uk

Jin-Ok-Shin

Dancing women on Thrunk

Jin-Ok-Shin

Flamingo

Jin-Ok-Shin
South Korea
schnoop@rogers.com

Rosa Sirvient

Details Menina

Materials: Paverpol Transparent, Pavercolor Brown, Art Stone, Wrappers, Plaster head, Porexpan-Origami and handmade paper, tin foil, Acrylic paint light flesh, ribbons, Lace, electrical wire

Menina (Spanish Maid of honour 1656)
By Velazquez

Rosa Sirvient
Spain
www.rosasirvient.es
rosa@rosasirvient.es

Sinelli

Mouse nest in Shoe

Sinelli
Finland
arja.varis@sinelli.fi

Riëtte Smit

Birdbuddy

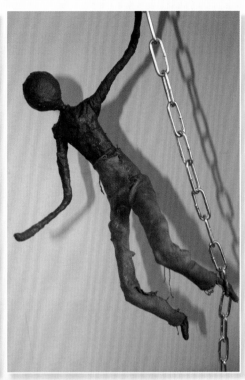

Materials: Paverpol Lead Grey, Paverplast, Pavercotton, Wrappers, tin foil, electrical wire, fabrics, Acrylic paints Yellow Ochre, Phythalo Blue, non rusting chain, fist size rock

Riëtte Smit

Susanne

Riëtte Smit
Netherlands
bijriette@kpnmail.nl

Two Ladies Sculpture

Materials Blue Dragon:
Paverpol Black and Bronze,
Pavercolor Blue, Silver, Bronze,
Gold, Stockinette, Black stretch
glitter fabrics, wooden base.

Blue Dragon

Lex Sorrentino

Paverpol Bra

Mask Wallhanging

Materials Mask: Paverpol
Transparent and Bronze,
Pavercolor Gold, canvas,
Burgundy leather, air dry clay

Mermaid Mirror

Lex Sorrentino
Australia
www.originalartdollsbylex.co
guslex@grapevine.net.au

Bird Cage Lady

Lise St-Cyr

Construction Bird Cage Lady

Materials: Paverpol Black and Bronze, Paverplast, Wrappers, Reliëfdecoration, Art Stone, Pavercolors Copper, Blue, Clear Blue, tin foil, air dry clay, empty wine bottle, tape, little bird cage

Lise St-Cyr
Canada
www.lisesaintcyr.com
lise.stcyr@gmail.com

Edina Szilardi

Edina Szilardi
Hungary
szilardie@freemail.hu

Shirley Tasker

Iris and Violet

Shirley Tasker

African Duo plus One

Melanie

Shirley Tasker
United Kingdom
shirley1@fsmail.net
www.stpaverpol.com

Merilyn Thomas

Catfish

Merilyn Thomas

Materials: Paverpol Transparent, Leopard print fabric, paint brush bristles to make the whiskers

Hanging Wall Mask

Materials: Paverpol Transparent, Pavercolor Stone Red, Copper wire, Glass Beads, Acrylic paint Copper

Merilyn Thomas
Australia
sculpturebymerilyn@hotmail.com
www.sculpturebymerilyn.com.au

Liliane van Tilborgh

Liliane van Tilborgh

Liliane van Tilborgh
Belgium
monnikenhofje@gmail.com
www.kunstpunt-vlaanderen.be/
kunstenaars-alfabethisch.html.

Brenda Topley

The Raven

Materials The Raven:
Paverpol Black, Art Stone,
Pavercolor Silver, tin foil, masking
tape, Josefine Varnish, cotton
T-shirt, Styrofoam balls, wire

The Mime-Getting out of the box

Materials The Mime: Paverpol Lead Grey,
Art Stone, Wrappers, Pavercolor Stone Red,
tin foil, masking tape, electrical wire, metal
pin, wooden base

Brenda Topley

Abigale

Materials: Paverpol Transparent, Paverplast, Pavercolors Antique Gold, Gold, Pavercotton, Wrappers, Reliëfdecoration, Josefine Varnish, tin foil, electrical wire, masking tape, metal pin

Brenda Topley
Canada
www.bstdesignstudio.com
info@bstdesignstudio.com

Jantina Tuthill

Jantina Tuthill
USA
www.paverpolusa.com
help@paverpolusa.com

Toos Vermeulen

Tsarina

Materials: Paverpol Black, Paverplast, Pavercotton, tin foil, metal pin with base, electrical wire, shells, earrings, old T-shirt, lace, Styrofoam egg, little Glass ball.

Toos Vermeulen

Little Girl in Ring

Materials: Paverpol Lead Grey and Black, Paverplast, Pavercotton, Styrofoam, or Straw ring, old T-shirt, lace, tin foil, electrical wire, little flowers, masking tape, Acrylic paint Silver, Raw Umber

Toos Vermeulen

Owl

Materials: Paverpol Bronze, Paverplast, electrical wire, tin foil, masking tape, Wrappers, Concrete base, metal pin, Styrofoam egg, Styrofoam ball, tree-stump, Acrylic paint Black, Raw Umber, Oxide Green, Veridean, Bronze

Toos Vermeulen
Netherlands
toosvermeulen@kpnplanet.nl

Elena Vylegzhanina

Elena Vylegzhanina
Russia
www.paverpol.ru
info@paverpol.ru

Suus van de Water

Paverpol Snail

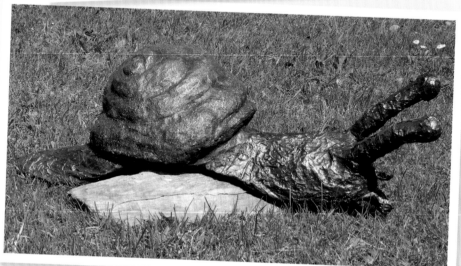

Materials: Paverpol Black, Art Stone, Paverplast, Styrofoam half ball, Styrofoam little balls, old T-shirt, Masking Tape, iron wire, Chicken wire, Paint Dark Brown and Gold, Varnis, flat stone

Suus van de Water
Netherlands
www.bijsuus.nl
info@bijsuus.nl

Harlinde Wieërs

Marilyn Monroe

Materials: Paverpol
Bronze, Paverplast,
Wrappers, mannequin,
half Styrofoam ball, cord,
old sheets, tin foil,
Acrylic paint White

Harlinde Wieërs

Sheep

Materials: Paverpol Black, Paverplast, tin foil, Styrofoam eggs, old cotton T-shirt, wool, electrical wire, bolts, screws

Harlinde Wieërs

Figurine with Cord

Materials: Paverpol Black and Bronze, Art Stone, Pavercotton, electrical wire, frame, Cord, Acrylic paint Gold and Orange

Harlinde Wieërs
Belgium
creafonie@gmail.com
www.creafonie.com

Iris Willems

Art Stone Object

Iris Willems

Ant

Iris Willems
Belgium
www.enjoytoday.be
iris@enjoytoday.be

Kim Willoughby

Kim Willoughby
Australia
kim002@bigpond.com

Helle Winther

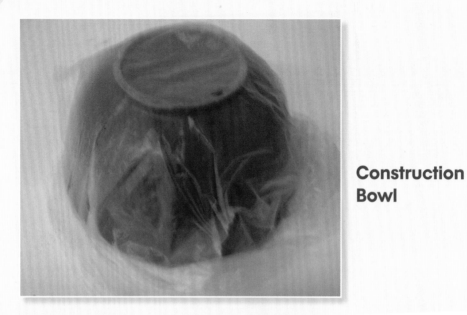

**Construction
Bowl**

Bowl

Helle Winther

Construction Halloween Lamp

Helle Winther
Denmark
www.art4me.dk
helleart4me@gmail.com

Monika Zilkova

Guardian Angel

Monika Zilkova

Monika Zilkova
Czech Republique
www.paverpol.sk
info@paverpol.sk

Wat is Paverpol vormpolymeer?

Paverpol vormpolymeer is ontwikkeld door een groep kunstenaars die er grote objecten mee maken. Het is een milieuvriendelijke vloeistof op waterbasis. Onschadelijk voor mens, dier en milieu. Paverpol vormpolymeer heeft het Amerikaanse AP veiligheidskeurmerk, zodat er op scholen en instellingen mee gewerkt kan worden.

Men kan met Paverpol vormpolymeer allerhande materialen keihard maken zoals textiel, papier maché, zeemleer, glasvezelmat, zelfhardende kleisoorten (geen synthetische) en vele natuurlijke materialen. Het laat zich hechten aan: hout, keramiek, gips, beton, steen en Styropor. Het hecht niet aan plastic.

Textiel moet in Paverpol vormpolymeer gedrenkt worden om een goede harding te krijgen. Het droogt snel aan de lucht. Hoe hoger de temperatuur, hoe sneller het droogt. De uitharding kan 1 á 2 weken duren.

Paverpol vormpolymeer kan gemengd worden met: papier maché, zaagsel, gips, cement, fijn zand etc.

Paverpol vormpolymeer is verkrijgbaar in transparant, zwart, loodkleur, brons en lichte huidskleur.

Bijproducten van Paverpol vormpolymeer zijn:
Pavercolors, om Paverpol transparant mee te kleuren.
Paverplast, om Paverpol mee te verdikken tot een pasta.
Art Stone poeder, om met Paverpol te mengen tot een klei.
Pavercotton, katoenen vezels, om pruikjes voor figuren mee te maken
Wrappers, dunne viscose doekjes, om in de Paverpol te drenken voor het omwikkelen van figuren, of voor decoratief gebruik op canvas doeken.
Stockinette, rekbare textiel, om in de Paverpol te drenken voor het aankleden, of decoreren van figuren.
Reliëfdecoration, gedroogde Berkenbast, om in de Paverpol te drenken voor allerhande decoratieve toepassingen.

Meer bijproducten en info op www.paverpol.com

What is Paverpol form polymer?

Paverpol form polymer was developed by a group of artists that wanted to create large objects. It is an environmentally-friendly, water-based liquid. It is completely harmless for humans, animals and the environment. Paverpol form polymer has received the American AP safety-standard mark. This means the material is safe for use in schools, etc.

The Paverpol form polymer can be used to harden all kinds of materials, such as: textile, papier-maché, chamois leather, glass-fibre mats, self-hardening types of clay (not synthetic) and all kinds of natural materials. It can be bond to: wood, ceramics, plaster, concrete, stone and Styropor. It does not bond to plastic.

The textile must be soaked in Paverpol form polymer to ensure that the material hardens properly. The material dries quickly in air. The higher the temperature, the faster it dries. It can take one to two weeks for the material to fully harden.

Paverpol form polymer can be mixed with: papier-maché, sawdust, plaster, cement, fine sand, etc.

Paverpol form polymer is available in transparent, black, lead colour, bronze and a light skin colour.

Paverpol form polymer can be mixed with other Paverpol products, such as:

Paver colours, to create a transparent Paverpol colour.

Paverplast, to thicken the Paverpol into a paste.

Art Stone powder to mix Paverpol into a clay.

Pavercotton (cotton fibre) to make wigs for figurines

Wrappers (thin viscose cloths) that are soaked in Paverpol and wrapped around the **figurines**, or can be used as decoration on canvas cloths.

Stockinette (elastic textile), this is soaked in Paverpol to dress or decorate figurines.

Relief decoration (dried birch bark), this is soaked in Paverpol and can be used for all kinds of decorative applications.

For more products and information, please go to www.paverpol.com

125

Paverpol importers list

AUSTRALIE
Paverpol Australia, Medowie NSW

AUSTRIA
Artlife sro, Nitra, Slovakia

BELGIUM
Dhondt Hobby, Desselgem

CANADA
Orange Wire Art, Chilliwack BC

CYPRUS
Charalambos Philippides & Son Ltd. Nicosia

DENMARK
Creativ Company, Holstebro

EAST EUROPE
(Albania, Bosnie Herzegowina, Bulgaria, Czech, Hungary, Kosova, Kroatie, Macedonie, Moldavy, Montenegro, Romania, Servie, Slovakia, Slovenie, Ukraine): Artlife sro,   Nitra, Slovakia

FINLAND
Sinelli oy Vantaa

FRANCE
MeLas, Commentry

GREECE
Carla Bellou, Viros, Corfu

IRELAND, NORTH IRELAND
Urney Creations, Strabane Co. Tyrone

ISRAEL
Tracey Lipman, Ramat Beit Shemesh

ITALY
Rosa Schiariti Importazioni, Capo d'Orlando (Messina)

MALTA
Krafty Hands, Zebbug

MEXICO
Fresh O2 Mexico SA, Cuauhtemoc, Mexico DF

NEW ZEALAND
Paverpol Australia Medowie NSW

POLAND
Mabeto, LOMIANKI

PORTUGAL
Sinache, Boadille Del Monte, Spain

RUSSIA, KAZACHSTAN & BELARUS
Elena Vylegzhanina, Ramenskoe, Moscow

SOUTH KOREA
Paverpol South Korea, Seoel

SPAIN
Sinache, Boadille Del Monte, Madrid

SURINAME
Printwise Imprint Solutions, Paramaribo

SWEDEN
Creativ Company, Holstebro Dk

SWITZERLAND
Art Atelier, Ottikon

UNITED KINGDOM
Paverpol-UK, Copthorne, West Sussex

UNITED STATES OF AMERICA
Paverpol USA LLP. Baltimore

Het groot stap-voor-stap

PAVERPOL boek

- 30 werkstukken en beschrijvingen -

Nederlands

PAVERPOL TEXTIELVERHARDER
voor kunstenaar en hobbyist

PAVERPOL TEXTILE HARDENER
for artist and hobbyist

The big book

"How to PAVERPOL"

English

- 30 pieces of works and descriptions -

Josefine

JOSSY DE ROODE